50 Premium Steak Cooking from Canada

By: Kelly Johnson

Table of Contents

- Classic Canadian Grilled Ribeye
- Maple-Glazed Striploin Steak
- Montreal-Style Peppercorn Steak
- Bison Ribeye with Wild Mushroom Sauce
- Whisky-Marinated Sirloin Steak
- Butter-Basted Filet Mignon
- Cedar-Plank Smoked Steak
- Garlic and Herb T-Bone Steak
- Canadian Beer-Marinated Flank Steak
- Espresso-Rubbed Striploin
- Chimichurri-Grilled Flat Iron Steak
- Honey-Mustard Glazed Skirt Steak
- Blue Cheese and Maple Steak Bites
- Smoked Prime Rib with Maple Rub
- Coffee-Crusted Ribeye
- Grilled Venison Steak with Red Wine Sauce
- Sweet and Spicy Maple Bourbon Steak
- Bison Sirloin with Wild Blueberry Reduction
- Classic Steak Diane
- Cast-Iron Seared Cowboy Steak
- Roasted Garlic and Herb Porterhouse Steak
- Saskatoon Berry BBQ Glazed Steak
- Beer-Braised Short Ribs
- Steak and Mushroom Poutine
- Teriyaki-Glazed Striploin
- Montreal Smoked Steak Sandwich
- Maple Butter-Basted Tomahawk Steak
- Steak with Roasted Bone Marrow Butter
- Garlic and Soy Marinated Skirt Steak
- Red Wine and Shallot Butter Steak
- Brown Sugar and Chipotle-Rubbed Sirloin
- Ginger-Sesame Flank Steak
- Steak au Poivre with Canadian Whisky
- BBQ Bison Steak with Smoky Maple Glaze
- Steak and Lobster Surf & Turf

- Grilled Hanger Steak with Caramelized Onions
- Roasted Poblano and Cheddar Stuffed Steak
- Applewood Smoked Striploin
- Charred Steak with Maple-Balsamic Glaze
- Bourbon and Maple Lacquered Steak
- Steak Frites with Herb Butter
- Black Garlic Butter Ribeye
- Steak Tacos with Maple Chipotle Sauce
- Grilled Steak with Horseradish Cream
- Rosemary and Thyme Butter-Basted Steak
- Steak with Wild Mushroom Cream Sauce
- Caramelized Onion and Cheddar Steak Melt
- Balsamic and Brown Sugar Glazed Steak
- Steak Skewers with Sweet Pepper Glaze
- Roasted Steak with Smoked Hickory Salt

Classic Canadian Grilled Ribeye

Ingredients:

- 2 ribeye steaks (1-inch thick)
- 2 tbsp olive oil
- 1 tsp sea salt
- 1/2 tsp black pepper
- 1 tsp fresh thyme, chopped

Instructions:

1. Preheat grill to high heat.
2. Rub steaks with olive oil, salt, pepper, and thyme.
3. Grill for 4-5 minutes per side for medium-rare.
4. Let rest for 5 minutes before serving.

Maple-Glazed Striploin Steak

Ingredients:

- 2 striploin steaks
- 1/4 cup pure maple syrup
- 1 tbsp Dijon mustard
- 1 tbsp soy sauce
- 1 tsp black pepper

Instructions:

1. In a bowl, whisk maple syrup, mustard, soy sauce, and black pepper.
2. Marinate steaks for 30 minutes.
3. Grill over medium-high heat for 4-5 minutes per side, brushing with glaze.
4. Let rest before serving.

Montreal-Style Peppercorn Steak

Ingredients:

- 2 striploin steaks
- 1 tbsp Montreal steak spice
- 1 tbsp cracked black pepper
- 1 tbsp olive oil

Instructions:

1. Rub steaks with oil, Montreal steak spice, and black pepper.
2. Let sit at room temperature for 30 minutes.
3. Grill over high heat for 4-5 minutes per side.
4. Rest for 5 minutes before serving.

Bison Ribeye with Wild Mushroom Sauce

Ingredients:

- 2 bison ribeye steaks
- 1 tbsp olive oil
- Salt and pepper to taste

Wild Mushroom Sauce:

- 1 cup mixed wild mushrooms, sliced
- 1 tbsp butter
- 1/2 cup beef broth
- 1/4 cup heavy cream
- 1 tsp fresh thyme

Instructions:

1. Heat grill to high and season bison steaks with salt, pepper, and olive oil.
2. Grill for 3-4 minutes per side for medium-rare.
3. In a pan, melt butter and sauté mushrooms until golden. Add broth, thyme, and reduce by half.
4. Stir in cream and simmer for 2 minutes. Serve over steak.

Whisky-Marinated Sirloin Steak

Ingredients:

- 2 sirloin steaks
- 1/4 cup whisky
- 2 tbsp soy sauce
- 1 tbsp brown sugar
- 1 tsp garlic powder

Instructions:

1. Mix whisky, soy sauce, brown sugar, and garlic powder. Marinate steaks for 1 hour.
2. Grill over medium-high heat for 4-5 minutes per side.
3. Rest for 5 minutes before serving.

Butter-Basted Filet Mignon

Ingredients:

- 2 filet mignon steaks
- 2 tbsp butter
- 2 cloves garlic, smashed
- 2 sprigs rosemary
- Salt and pepper to taste

Instructions:

1. Preheat a cast-iron skillet over high heat. Season steaks with salt and pepper.
2. Sear steaks for 2 minutes per side. Add butter, garlic, and rosemary.
3. Baste steaks with melted butter for 1-2 minutes.
4. Rest for 5 minutes before serving.

Cedar-Plank Smoked Steak

Ingredients:

- 2 ribeye or striploin steaks
- 1 cedar plank (soaked in water for 1 hour)
- 1 tbsp olive oil
- 1 tsp sea salt
- 1/2 tsp smoked paprika

Instructions:

1. Preheat grill to medium heat.
2. Rub steaks with oil, salt, and smoked paprika.
3. Place steaks on the cedar plank and grill for 10-12 minutes until medium-rare.
4. Rest before serving.

Garlic and Herb T-Bone Steak

Ingredients:

- 2 T-bone steaks
- 2 tbsp olive oil
- 3 cloves garlic, minced
- 1 tbsp chopped rosemary
- 1 tsp salt
- 1/2 tsp black pepper

Instructions:

1. Rub steaks with olive oil, garlic, rosemary, salt, and pepper.
2. Let sit at room temperature for 30 minutes.
3. Grill over high heat for 5-6 minutes per side.
4. Rest before serving.

Canadian Beer-Marinated Flank Steak

Ingredients:

- 1 flank steak
- 1/2 cup Canadian beer
- 2 tbsp soy sauce
- 1 tbsp Dijon mustard
- 1 tsp garlic powder

Instructions:

1. Mix beer, soy sauce, mustard, and garlic powder. Marinate steak for 1-2 hours.
2. Grill over high heat for 4-5 minutes per side.
3. Rest for 5 minutes before slicing against the grain.

Espresso-Rubbed Striploin

Ingredients:

- 2 striploin steaks
- 2 tbsp finely ground espresso
- 1 tsp brown sugar
- 1 tsp smoked paprika
- 1/2 tsp salt
- 1/2 tsp black pepper
- 1 tbsp olive oil

Instructions:

1. Mix espresso, brown sugar, paprika, salt, and pepper.
2. Rub mixture onto steaks and let sit for 30 minutes.
3. Heat grill or skillet over high heat. Drizzle steaks with olive oil and grill for 4-5 minutes per side.
4. Rest for 5 minutes before serving.

Chimichurri-Grilled Flat Iron Steak

Ingredients:

Steak:

- 1 flat iron steak
- 1 tbsp olive oil
- Salt and black pepper to taste

Chimichurri Sauce:

- 1/2 cup fresh parsley, chopped
- 2 tbsp red wine vinegar
- 2 cloves garlic, minced
- 1/4 tsp red pepper flakes
- 1/3 cup olive oil
- Salt and pepper to taste

Instructions:

1. Mix chimichurri ingredients in a bowl and let sit for 15 minutes.
2. Season steak with salt, pepper, and olive oil. Grill over medium-high heat for 3-4 minutes per side.
3. Rest for 5 minutes, slice against the grain, and serve with chimichurri sauce.

Honey-Mustard Glazed Skirt Steak

Ingredients:

- 1 skirt steak
- 1/4 cup honey
- 2 tbsp Dijon mustard
- 1 tbsp soy sauce
- 1 tsp garlic powder

Instructions:

1. Whisk honey, mustard, soy sauce, and garlic powder. Marinate steak for 1 hour.
2. Grill over high heat for 3 minutes per side.
3. Let rest, then slice against the grain before serving.

Blue Cheese and Maple Steak Bites

Ingredients:

- 1 lb sirloin or ribeye steak, cubed
- 1 tbsp olive oil
- 1/2 tsp salt
- 1/2 tsp black pepper
- 1/4 cup crumbled blue cheese
- 1 tbsp pure maple syrup

Instructions:

1. Heat olive oil in a skillet over medium-high heat.
2. Season steak bites with salt and pepper, then sear for 2-3 minutes per side.
3. Drizzle with maple syrup and toss.
4. Remove from heat and sprinkle with blue cheese before serving.

Smoked Prime Rib with Maple Rub

Ingredients:

- 1 bone-in prime rib roast (4-5 lbs)
- 1/4 cup pure maple syrup
- 1 tbsp sea salt
- 1 tbsp black pepper
- 1 tbsp smoked paprika
- 1 tsp garlic powder

Instructions:

1. Rub prime rib with maple syrup, salt, pepper, paprika, and garlic powder. Let sit for 1 hour.
2. Preheat smoker to 225°F (110°C).
3. Smoke for 3-4 hours until internal temp reaches 130°F (54°C) for medium-rare.
4. Let rest for 20 minutes before slicing.

Coffee-Crusted Ribeye

Ingredients:

- 2 ribeye steaks
- 2 tbsp finely ground coffee
- 1 tsp brown sugar
- 1 tsp black pepper
- 1/2 tsp sea salt
- 1 tbsp olive oil

Instructions:

1. Mix coffee, brown sugar, pepper, and salt. Rub onto steaks and let sit for 30 minutes.
2. Heat grill or skillet to high heat and sear steaks for 4-5 minutes per side.
3. Rest for 5 minutes before serving.

Grilled Venison Steak with Red Wine Sauce

Ingredients:

Steak:

- 2 venison steaks
- 1 tbsp olive oil
- Salt and black pepper to taste

Red Wine Sauce:

- 1/2 cup red wine
- 1/4 cup beef broth
- 1 shallot, minced
- 1 tbsp butter

Instructions:

1. Heat grill to medium-high. Rub venison with olive oil, salt, and pepper.
2. Grill for 3-4 minutes per side. Rest before serving.
3. In a pan, sauté shallots in butter. Add wine and broth, simmer until reduced.
4. Drizzle sauce over steak before serving.

Sweet and Spicy Maple Bourbon Steak

Ingredients:

- 2 New York strip steaks
- 1/4 cup bourbon
- 2 tbsp pure maple syrup
- 1 tbsp soy sauce
- 1 tsp crushed red pepper flakes
- 1/2 tsp salt

Instructions:

1. Mix bourbon, maple syrup, soy sauce, red pepper flakes, and salt. Marinate steaks for 1 hour.
2. Grill over high heat for 4-5 minutes per side.
3. Let rest before serving.

Bison Sirloin with Wild Blueberry Reduction

Ingredients:

Steak:

- 2 bison sirloin steaks
- 1 tbsp olive oil
- Salt and black pepper to taste

Wild Blueberry Sauce:

- 1/2 cup wild blueberries
- 1/4 cup red wine
- 1 tbsp maple syrup
- 1 tsp balsamic vinegar

Instructions:

1. Heat grill to high. Rub bison with olive oil, salt, and pepper.
2. Grill for 3-4 minutes per side. Rest before serving.
3. In a saucepan, heat blueberries, wine, maple syrup, and balsamic vinegar. Simmer until reduced.
4. Spoon sauce over steak before serving.

Classic Steak Diane

Ingredients:

- 2 filet mignon steaks
- 1 tbsp butter
- 1 shallot, minced
- 1/4 cup beef broth
- 1/4 cup heavy cream
- 2 tbsp Worcestershire sauce
- 1 tbsp Dijon mustard
- 1 tbsp brandy (optional)

Instructions:

1. Sear steaks in butter for 3 minutes per side. Remove and set aside.
2. In the same pan, sauté shallots, then add broth, Worcestershire, Dijon, and brandy. Simmer for 2 minutes.
3. Stir in heavy cream and return steaks to the pan. Simmer for 1 minute.
4. Serve with sauce drizzled over top.

Cast-Iron Seared Cowboy Steak

Ingredients:

- 1 cowboy-cut bone-in ribeye steak (2-inch thick)
- 2 tbsp olive oil
- 2 tbsp butter
- 2 cloves garlic, smashed
- 2 sprigs rosemary
- Salt and black pepper to taste

Instructions:

1. Preheat oven to 400°F (200°C).
2. Heat a cast-iron skillet over high heat. Rub steak with olive oil, salt, and black pepper.
3. Sear steak for 2 minutes per side. Add butter, garlic, and rosemary, basting the steak.
4. Transfer skillet to the oven and cook for 5-7 minutes for medium-rare.
5. Rest for 10 minutes before slicing.

Roasted Garlic and Herb Porterhouse Steak

Ingredients:

- 1 large Porterhouse steak
- 1 tbsp olive oil
- 4 cloves roasted garlic, mashed
- 1 tbsp fresh rosemary, chopped
- 1 tbsp fresh thyme, chopped
- Salt and black pepper to taste

Instructions:

1. Preheat grill to high heat.
2. Mix olive oil, roasted garlic, rosemary, thyme, salt, and pepper. Rub onto the steak.
3. Grill steak for 5-6 minutes per side for medium-rare.
4. Let rest for 10 minutes before serving.

Saskatoon Berry BBQ Glazed Steak

Ingredients:

- 2 striploin steaks
- 1/2 cup Saskatoon berries
- 1/4 cup ketchup
- 2 tbsp maple syrup
- 1 tbsp apple cider vinegar
- 1 tsp smoked paprika

Instructions:

1. In a saucepan, combine Saskatoon berries, ketchup, maple syrup, vinegar, and paprika. Simmer for 10 minutes, then blend until smooth.
2. Season steaks with salt and pepper, then grill for 4-5 minutes per side.
3. Brush with Saskatoon BBQ glaze in the last 2 minutes of cooking.
4. Let rest before serving.

Beer-Braised Short Ribs

Ingredients:

- 2 lbs beef short ribs
- 1 bottle Canadian beer
- 1 cup beef broth
- 1 onion, chopped
- 3 cloves garlic, minced
- 2 tbsp tomato paste
- 1 tbsp Worcestershire sauce
- 1 tsp salt
- 1/2 tsp black pepper

Instructions:

1. Preheat oven to 325°F (165°C).
2. Season short ribs with salt and pepper, then sear in a Dutch oven until browned.
3. Remove ribs, then sauté onions and garlic. Stir in tomato paste, beer, and broth.
4. Return ribs to the pot, cover, and braise in the oven for 2.5-3 hours until tender.

Steak and Mushroom Poutine

Ingredients:

- 1 lb sirloin steak
- 2 russet potatoes, cut into fries
- 1 cup cheese curds
- 1 cup mushrooms, sliced
- 1 cup beef gravy
- 2 tbsp butter
- Salt and pepper to taste

Instructions:

1. Cook fries in hot oil at 375°F (190°C) until crispy. Drain and season with salt.
2. Sear steak in butter for 4-5 minutes per side. Let rest, then slice thinly.
3. Sauté mushrooms in butter.
4. Layer fries, steak, mushrooms, and cheese curds. Pour hot gravy over top and serve.

Teriyaki-Glazed Striploin

Ingredients:

- 2 striploin steaks
- 1/4 cup soy sauce
- 2 tbsp honey
- 1 tbsp rice vinegar
- 1 tsp sesame oil
- 1 tsp ginger, grated

Instructions:

1. Mix soy sauce, honey, rice vinegar, sesame oil, and ginger. Marinate steaks for 1 hour.
2. Grill over medium-high heat for 4-5 minutes per side, brushing with marinade.
3. Rest before serving.

Montreal Smoked Steak Sandwich

Ingredients:

- 1 lb Montreal smoked meat, sliced
- 4 slices rye bread
- 2 tbsp yellow mustard
- 4 slices Swiss cheese

Instructions:

1. Steam smoked meat for 10 minutes to warm it.
2. Spread mustard on rye bread, add meat and Swiss cheese.
3. Toast sandwich in a pan until cheese melts.

Maple Butter-Basted Tomahawk Steak

Ingredients:

- 1 tomahawk steak (bone-in ribeye)
- 2 tbsp butter
- 1 tbsp pure maple syrup
- 2 cloves garlic, smashed
- Salt and black pepper to taste

Instructions:

1. Preheat grill to high heat.
2. Season steak with salt and pepper. Grill for 5-6 minutes per side.
3. In the last 2 minutes, baste with butter, maple syrup, and garlic.
4. Let rest before slicing.

Steak with Roasted Bone Marrow Butter

Ingredients:

Steak:

- 2 ribeye steaks
- 1 tbsp olive oil
- Salt and pepper to taste

Bone Marrow Butter:

- 2 marrow bones, roasted
- 2 tbsp butter
- 1 tsp chopped parsley

Instructions:

1. Roast marrow bones at 450°F (230°C) for 15 minutes, then scoop out marrow and mix with butter and parsley.
2. Grill steaks for 4-5 minutes per side.
3. Top steaks with bone marrow butter before serving.

Garlic and Soy Marinated Skirt Steak

Ingredients:

- 1 skirt steak
- 1/4 cup soy sauce
- 1 tbsp honey
- 1 tbsp sesame oil
- 3 cloves garlic, minced

Instructions:

1. Mix soy sauce, honey, sesame oil, and garlic. Marinate steak for 1 hour.
2. Grill over high heat for 3-4 minutes per side.
3. Rest before slicing against the grain.

Red Wine and Shallot Butter Steak

Ingredients:

- 2 ribeye or filet mignon steaks
- 2 tbsp olive oil
- Salt and black pepper to taste

Shallot Butter:

- 2 tbsp butter, softened
- 1 small shallot, finely minced
- 1/4 cup red wine
- 1 tsp fresh thyme

Instructions:

1. Heat a skillet over high heat. Rub steaks with oil, salt, and pepper.
2. Sear for 4-5 minutes per side for medium-rare. Rest for 5 minutes.
3. In the same skillet, sauté shallots until soft, then deglaze with red wine. Simmer until reduced, then mix with softened butter and thyme.
4. Serve steaks with shallot butter on top.

Brown Sugar and Chipotle-Rubbed Sirloin

Ingredients:

- 2 sirloin steaks
- 2 tbsp brown sugar
- 1 tsp chipotle powder
- 1/2 tsp smoked paprika
- 1/2 tsp salt
- 1/2 tsp black pepper
- 1 tbsp olive oil

Instructions:

1. Mix brown sugar, chipotle powder, paprika, salt, and pepper.
2. Rub steaks with olive oil and spice mixture. Let sit for 30 minutes.
3. Grill over medium-high heat for 4-5 minutes per side.
4. Rest for 5 minutes before serving.

Ginger-Sesame Flank Steak

Ingredients:

- 1 flank steak
- 1/4 cup soy sauce
- 2 tbsp sesame oil
- 1 tbsp grated ginger
- 2 cloves garlic, minced
- 1 tbsp honey

Instructions:

1. Whisk soy sauce, sesame oil, ginger, garlic, and honey. Marinate steak for 1 hour.
2. Grill over high heat for 3-4 minutes per side.
3. Let rest before slicing against the grain.

Steak au Poivre with Canadian Whisky

Ingredients:

- 2 filet mignon steaks
- 2 tbsp black peppercorns, crushed
- 1 tbsp olive oil
- 1/2 cup Canadian whisky
- 1/2 cup heavy cream
- 1 tbsp Dijon mustard

Instructions:

1. Press crushed peppercorns into steaks.
2. Sear steaks in oil over high heat for 4 minutes per side. Remove and set aside.
3. Deglaze pan with whisky, then stir in cream and Dijon mustard. Simmer for 2 minutes.
4. Return steaks to pan, coat with sauce, and serve.

BBQ Bison Steak with Smoky Maple Glaze

Ingredients:

- 2 bison steaks
- 1/4 cup pure maple syrup
- 1 tbsp smoked paprika
- 1 tbsp apple cider vinegar
- 1 tsp garlic powder

Instructions:

1. Mix maple syrup, paprika, vinegar, and garlic powder.
2. Brush steaks with glaze and let marinate for 30 minutes.
3. Grill over medium-high heat for 4-5 minutes per side.
4. Rest before serving.

Steak and Lobster Surf & Turf

Ingredients:

- 2 filet mignon steaks
- 2 lobster tails
- 2 tbsp butter, melted
- 1 tbsp lemon juice
- 1 tsp garlic, minced

Instructions:

1. Grill steaks for 4-5 minutes per side.
2. Split lobster tails and brush with butter, lemon juice, and garlic.
3. Grill lobster flesh-side down for 4 minutes.
4. Serve steaks with grilled lobster and extra butter.

Grilled Hanger Steak with Caramelized Onions

Ingredients:

- 1 hanger steak
- 1 tbsp olive oil
- Salt and black pepper to taste

Caramelized Onions:

- 1 large onion, thinly sliced
- 1 tbsp butter
- 1 tsp balsamic vinegar

Instructions:

1. Heat butter in a pan and sauté onions until golden brown (about 15 minutes). Stir in balsamic vinegar and set aside.
2. Rub steak with olive oil, salt, and pepper. Grill over high heat for 3-4 minutes per side.
3. Slice steak and top with caramelized onions.

Roasted Poblano and Cheddar Stuffed Steak

Ingredients:

- 2 thick-cut sirloin steaks
- 1 roasted poblano pepper, sliced
- 1/2 cup shredded cheddar cheese
- 1 tbsp olive oil
- Salt and pepper to taste

Instructions:

1. Cut a pocket into each steak. Stuff with poblano slices and cheddar.
2. Secure with toothpicks and season with salt, pepper, and olive oil.
3. Grill over medium heat for 5-6 minutes per side. Rest before serving.

Applewood Smoked Striploin

Ingredients:

- 2 striploin steaks
- 1 tbsp olive oil
- 1 tsp smoked sea salt
- 1/2 tsp black pepper
- Applewood chips for smoking

Instructions:

1. Soak applewood chips in water for 30 minutes.
2. Rub steaks with oil, smoked salt, and pepper.
3. Place steaks on the grill over indirect heat with applewood chips smoking.
4. Smoke for 30 minutes at 225°F (110°C), then sear over high heat for 1-2 minutes per side.

Charred Steak with Maple-Balsamic Glaze

Ingredients:

- 2 ribeye steaks
- 1/4 cup balsamic vinegar
- 2 tbsp pure maple syrup
- 1 tsp Dijon mustard

Instructions:

1. Mix balsamic vinegar, maple syrup, and Dijon mustard.
2. Brush steaks with glaze and let sit for 20 minutes.
3. Grill over high heat for 4-5 minutes per side, charring slightly.
4. Let rest before serving.

Bourbon and Maple Lacquered Steak

Ingredients:

- 2 New York strip steaks
- 1/4 cup bourbon
- 2 tbsp maple syrup
- 1 tbsp soy sauce
- 1/2 tsp smoked paprika

Instructions:

1. Mix bourbon, maple syrup, soy sauce, and smoked paprika. Marinate steaks for 1 hour.
2. Grill over medium-high heat for 4-5 minutes per side, brushing with extra marinade.
3. Rest before serving.

Steak Frites with Herb Butter

Ingredients:

Steak:

- 2 striploin or ribeye steaks
- 1 tbsp olive oil
- Salt and black pepper to taste

Frites:

- 2 large russet potatoes, cut into fries
- 2 tbsp vegetable oil
- Salt to taste

Herb Butter:

- 3 tbsp butter, softened
- 1 tbsp fresh parsley, chopped
- 1 tsp fresh thyme, chopped
- 1 clove garlic, minced

Instructions:

1. Mix butter, parsley, thyme, and garlic. Refrigerate until firm.
2. Toss fries with oil and bake at 425°F (220°C) for 30 minutes, flipping halfway.
3. Heat grill or pan to high heat. Rub steaks with oil, salt, and pepper.
4. Grill steaks for 4-5 minutes per side. Rest for 5 minutes.
5. Serve steaks topped with herb butter alongside crispy fries.

Black Garlic Butter Ribeye

Ingredients:

- 2 ribeye steaks
- 1 tbsp olive oil
- Salt and black pepper to taste

Black Garlic Butter:

- 3 tbsp butter, softened
- 2 cloves black garlic, mashed
- 1 tsp soy sauce

Instructions:

1. Mix black garlic, butter, and soy sauce. Refrigerate until firm.
2. Heat grill or pan to high heat. Season steaks with oil, salt, and pepper.
3. Grill steaks for 4-5 minutes per side. Rest for 5 minutes.
4. Serve steaks with a dollop of black garlic butter.

Steak Tacos with Maple Chipotle Sauce

Ingredients:

Steak:

- 1 lb flank steak
- 1 tbsp olive oil
- 1/2 tsp salt
- 1/2 tsp black pepper

Maple Chipotle Sauce:

- 2 tbsp pure maple syrup
- 1 tbsp chipotle paste
- 1 tbsp lime juice

Tacos:

- 8 small corn tortillas
- 1/2 cup chopped cilantro
- 1/4 cup diced red onion

Instructions:

1. Mix maple syrup, chipotle paste, and lime juice. Set aside.
2. Rub steak with oil, salt, and pepper. Grill over high heat for 4 minutes per side.
3. Let rest for 5 minutes, then slice thinly.
4. Warm tortillas and fill with steak slices. Drizzle with sauce and top with cilantro and red onion.

Grilled Steak with Horseradish Cream

Ingredients:

- 2 sirloin steaks
- 1 tbsp olive oil
- Salt and black pepper to taste

Horseradish Cream:

- 1/2 cup sour cream
- 1 tbsp prepared horseradish
- 1 tsp lemon juice
- Salt and pepper to taste

Instructions:

1. Mix horseradish cream ingredients and refrigerate.
2. Heat grill to high heat. Season steaks with oil, salt, and pepper.
3. Grill steaks for 4-5 minutes per side. Rest for 5 minutes.
4. Serve with a dollop of horseradish cream.

Rosemary and Thyme Butter-Basted Steak

Ingredients:

- 2 filet mignon or ribeye steaks
- 2 tbsp butter
- 2 cloves garlic, smashed
- 1 sprig rosemary
- 1 sprig thyme
- Salt and black pepper to taste

Instructions:

1. Heat a cast-iron skillet over high heat. Season steaks with salt and pepper.
2. Sear steaks for 2 minutes per side. Add butter, garlic, rosemary, and thyme.
3. Baste steaks with melted butter for 1-2 minutes.
4. Rest for 5 minutes before serving.

Steak with Wild Mushroom Cream Sauce

Ingredients:

Steak:

- 2 sirloin or ribeye steaks
- 1 tbsp olive oil
- Salt and black pepper to taste

Wild Mushroom Cream Sauce:

- 1 cup mixed wild mushrooms, sliced
- 1 tbsp butter
- 1/2 cup heavy cream
- 1/4 cup beef broth
- 1 tsp fresh thyme

Instructions:

1. Heat grill or pan to high heat. Rub steaks with oil, salt, and pepper.
2. Grill steaks for 4-5 minutes per side. Rest for 5 minutes.
3. In a pan, melt butter and sauté mushrooms. Add broth, thyme, and cream. Simmer until thickened.
4. Serve steaks topped with mushroom sauce.

Caramelized Onion and Cheddar Steak Melt

Ingredients:

- 2 sirloin steaks
- 1 tbsp olive oil
- Salt and black pepper to taste

Toppings:

- 1 large onion, sliced
- 1 tbsp butter
- 4 slices sharp cheddar cheese
- 4 slices sourdough bread

Instructions:

1. Heat a pan over medium heat. Sauté onions in butter until golden brown.
2. Grill steaks for 4-5 minutes per side. Rest and slice thinly.
3. Assemble sandwiches with steak, onions, and cheese.
4. Toast on a skillet until golden brown.

Balsamic and Brown Sugar Glazed Steak

Ingredients:

- 2 ribeye or striploin steaks
- 1/4 cup balsamic vinegar
- 2 tbsp brown sugar
- 1 tbsp Dijon mustard

Instructions:

1. Mix balsamic vinegar, brown sugar, and Dijon mustard.
2. Brush onto steaks and let sit for 20 minutes.
3. Grill over medium-high heat for 4-5 minutes per side, brushing with glaze.
4. Rest before serving.

Steak Skewers with Sweet Pepper Glaze

Ingredients:

- 1 lb sirloin steak, cubed
- 1 red bell pepper, cubed
- 1 yellow bell pepper, cubed
- 1 tbsp olive oil
- Salt and black pepper to taste

Sweet Pepper Glaze:

- 1/4 cup honey
- 1 tbsp soy sauce
- 1 tsp smoked paprika

Instructions:

1. Mix honey, soy sauce, and smoked paprika.
2. Thread steak and peppers onto skewers. Brush with oil, salt, and pepper.
3. Grill for 3-4 minutes per side, brushing with glaze.

Roasted Steak with Smoked Hickory Salt

Ingredients:

- 2 striploin or ribeye steaks
- 1 tbsp olive oil
- 1 tsp smoked hickory salt
- 1/2 tsp black pepper

Instructions:

1. Preheat oven to 400°F (200°C).
2. Rub steaks with olive oil, smoked hickory salt, and black pepper.
3. Sear steaks in a hot pan for 2 minutes per side.
4. Transfer to oven and roast for 5-7 minutes for medium-rare.
5. Rest before serving.

www.ingramcontent.com/pod-product-compliance
Lightning Source LLC
LaVergne TN
LVHW081501060526
838201LV00056BA/2868